OPA & OMA TOGETHER

Story by Patrick "Packy" Mader

Illustrated by Andrew Holmquist

Beaver's Pond Press, Inc.

ISBN-13: 978-1-59298-120-5
ISBN-10: 1-59298-120-8

Library of Congress Catalog Number: 2005906663

Printed in the United States of America

First Printing: August 2005
Second Printing: February 2006

09 08 07 06   5 4 3 2

Special thanks to Mary Jo Mader Franske whose detailed photographs served as a source for many of the illustrations.
Edited by Catherine Friend.
Project management and publishing advice provided by Kellie Hultgren, Beaver's Pond Press.
Layout, formatting and typesetting by Mori Studio, Inc.

Beaver's Pond Press, Inc.

7104 Ohms Lane, Suite 216
Edina, MN 55439
(952) 829-8818
www.BeaversPondPress.com

To order, visit www.BookHouseFulfillment.com
or call 1-800-901-3480. Reseller discounts available.

DEDICATIONS

To George and Mary Margaret (Schultes) Mader

known to many as Opa and Oma

—and—

Karen, Karl, and Ellen

you enrich my life daily

P.M.

To Dad and Mom

A.H.

This is Opa. He lives on a farm in Minnesota. He loves the land.

This is Oma. She lives on the farm with Opa. She loves the home.

Opa is a German word for Grandpa.

Oma is a German word for Grandma.

Sometimes they still speak German to their sixteen grandchildren.

After Opa and Oma married, they moved to their farm.
They proudly walked around the land and the home.

They were growing in life…

Together.

Soon they had cows, pigs, and chickens on the farm. They always had a dog and many cats.

And they had seven children.

Sometimes the cows mooed, the pigs squealed, the chickens squawked, the dog barked, the cats screeched, and the tractors roared—all at the same time.

And always one child seemed to be shouting, **"I'm hungry!"**

It was a very noisy place!

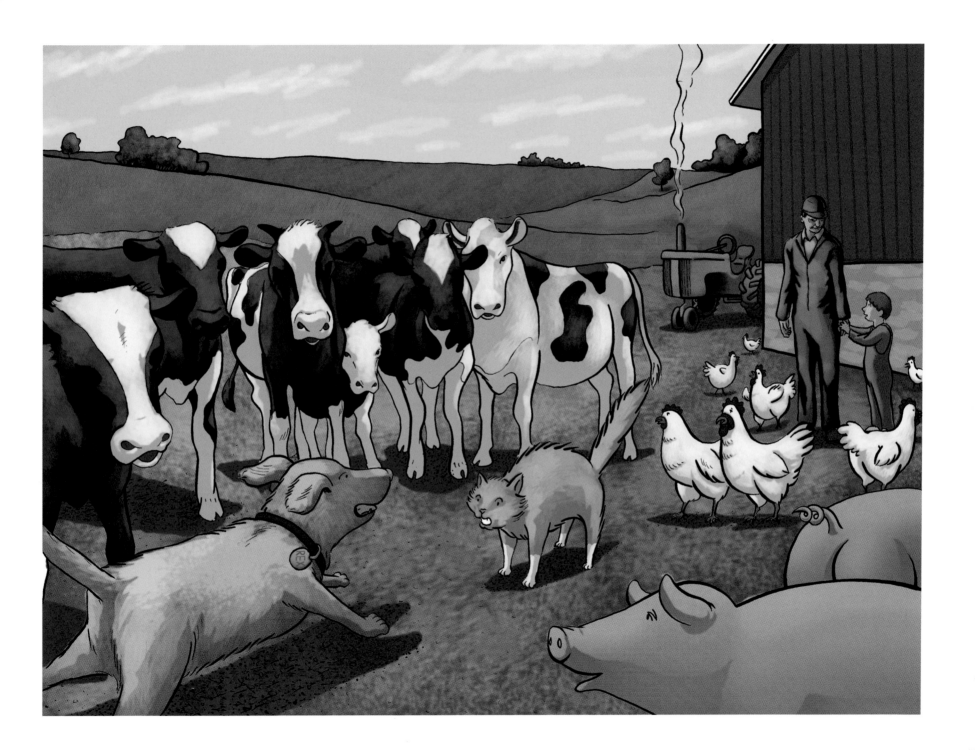

Opa would get up very early every morning to feed the animals and milk the cows. He would plant corn and oat seeds. Then he would take care of the plants until they were ready to be harvested.

Oma would also get up very early every morning to bake bread, doughnuts, and cookies, take care of the seven children, sew and quilt, and make the home warm and welcoming.

Sometimes Opa and Oma would take a walk through the fields of corn or hay and look at the plants. Like the plants, they were growing in life…

Together.

Opa and Oma not only watched the plants grow in the fields. They not only helped nurture and shape the crops and newborn calves.

They also watched their seven children grow on the farm and in the home. They helped nurture and shape the lives of their children.

The children grew and learned and traveled. They remembered the lessons from the farm and the home.

One by one, they moved away. They began jobs, got married, and had their own children.

Now none of them live on a farm.

But the seven children and their families come back to the farm to visit Opa and Oma often. And they remember the lessons they learned from the farm and the home.

Opa and Oma's grandchildren are now learning those same lessons. They are planting seeds and caring for animals.

They love the farm and the home.

With the children now gone, the farm is quiet. The cows, pigs, and chickens are now gone too.

But Opa and Oma are still on the farm and in the home.

Opa does not farm any more. Instead he has four gardens, so he is still taking care of plants. And he takes care of cats and, sometimes, a dog.

Oma does not take care of seven children any more. Instead she has sixteen grandchildren. She still makes a warm and welcoming home. She sews and quilts more often… for the grandchildren. She still bakes bread, doughnuts, and cookies… for the grandchildren.

Now, when Opa and Oma walk through the gardens, Opa's back is very bent and Oma's legs move slowly. But they still look at the plants and see how they are growing. They have berries, pumpkins, watermelons, sunflowers, tomatoes, potatoes, and much more. Their grandchildren love picking and tasting the berries the best.

After fifty years, as they walk the same farm with the same home, Opa and Oma are still growing in life…

Together.